the Syrian Leper

E. P. ROGERS

BAKER BOOK HOUSE
Grand Rapids, Michigan

Paperback edition issued 1977
by Baker Book House
ISBN: 0-8010-7655-2

PHOTOLITHOPRINTED BY CUSHING - MALLOY, INC.
ANN ARBOR, MICHIGAN, UNITED STATES OF AMERICA
1977

CONTENTS

THE SYRIAN LEPER ---------------------PAGE 5

THE CAPTIVE MAID--------------------------- 24

THE CURE SOUGHT--------------------------- 43

THE WRONG WAY----------------------------- 62

THE LEPER HEALED ------------------------- 79

THE SYRIAN LEPER

———— •◦• ————

Now Naaman, captain of the host of the king of Syria,
was a great man with his master, and honorable, because
by him the Lord had given deliverance unto Syria ; he was
also a mighty man in valor ; but he was a leper. 2 KINGS 5:1.

THERE is scarcely any one of the
narratives of the Bible more
celebrated than this. The simple, graphic style of the story itself;
the interesting nature of the incidents
which it records; and the variety and
importance of the lessons which it teaches, all conspire to give it a prominent
place in the Old Testament history. In
fact, it occupies a place in the Old Testament very similar to that held by the
beautiful parable of the Prodigal Son in

the New, and there is much that is alike
in the instruction which they contain.

The character presented to us in this
story is that of an individual around
whom Providence seems to have thrown
an unusual array of advantages. His
position was one of the highest in the
kingdom; he was the favorite of his
king; he was the commander-in-chief of
the royal forces. All the honors and
emoluments which belonged to such illustrious rank were his; and not only so,
but he also enjoyed the fame of being a
brave and successful general. There is
scarcely any position more distinguished
than this. Scenes of battle and grand
campaigns have always had great interest for men, and a successful general is
the popular idol. It is so, even in this
age when it might be supposed that in-
tellectual and moral forces would have
the preëminence in the regard of men.

But in that early age, more an age of
force and physical prowess, a great general must have been a distinguished personage. So Naaman stood apparently
on the summit of human greatness, and
seems to us to have been in a most en-
viable position.

And yet, probably, the meanest slave
in all Syria would have scorned to change
places with him. With all his greatness,
his fame, and his wealth, there is one
unhappy drawback that vitiates it all,
and makes this great man the scorn and
pity of the lowest in the kingdom. He
was captain of the host of the king of
Syria; he was a great man with his master, and honorable; he was a mighty
man of valor, and a victor in many a
field; BUT *he was a leper*.

To understand fully the significance of
this dreadful *but*, which qualifies the
glowing description of this great man's

position, we ought to know what a loathsome and horrible disease the oriental leprosy was. Yet the details are so shocking that you must excuse me from spreading them before you. The disease is spoken of under four different heads: the leprosy of the Greeks, the Jews, the Arabians, and the leprosy of the Middle Ages. That which is mentioned in the Scriptures is the leprosy of the Jews, and it seems to have prevailed extensively in India and the neighborhood. It is very evident, from the many and minute directions given in the Mosaic law for the treatment of those who were affected with this malady, that it inspired the greatest horror and disgust in the people, and that a most rigid system of exclusion was enforced, by which the leper was generally shut out from his race, obliged to wear a peculiar dress, to give warning of his vicinity to any unconscious traveller, and was considered as a polluted man— suspended from society, and under the curse of God.

The great idea which pervaded the legislation of the Hebrew economy was that the people were the Lord's; that every thing belonging to them, even their bodies, were to be holy unto God. They were to be in all respects a separated people. The stamp of God's ownership was to be applied to them, and thus their ritual was crowded with an immense variety of ceremonial ordinances, which related to outward purity, and which were obligatory on the whole nation. In the case of the leper, it almost seems as if the legislation was such as to convey the idea of a death in the eye of the law. And the unfortunate man, with uncovered head and rent garments, uttering the mournful cry, "Unclean, unclean," avoided and dreaded by all, presents a picture of misery which appeals to our pity, even while it provokes our disgust.

There were exceptions to this rigorous treatment of the leper, as in the case of Gehazi, the servant of the prophet, and of the lepers in the camp at Samaria, as well as those mentioned in the history of our Lord; but we can readily see how terrible an affliction, how intolerable and revolting a stain was this foul disease in every case; and we can understand something of the fearful force of that little word when it is said Naaman was a great man, honorable, captain of the royal host, and a mighty man of valor, BUT he was a leper. All his greatness could neither conceal nor remove this foul blot. Wherever he went, he carried the plague-spot with him. He was a leper, a pariah, an object of miserable pity, of unconcealed disgust. He lay down at night; he rose in the morning; he walked forth in the day; he stood in the court of the king; he rode at the head of the army—and the miserable consciousness of this dreadful blot upon his body never left him for a moment.

You can conceive of the grinding pressure of such a thought to a proud and sensitive spirit. It is said that Byron's misshapen foot was a life-long source of annoyance and humiliation to him; but the leprosy was worse than any deformity: it ultimately made the whole body a loathsome and disgusting mass; it was a living death, and well might the unfortunate victim cry out in the very words of Paul, "Oh, wretched man that I am! Who shall deliver me from the body of this death?" Who in all the kingdom of Syria would have exchang-

ed places with Naaman? What were all
his wealth, and rank, and power worth
with that fatal plague-spot with its
ghastly whiteness, on his face? As he
rode through the ranks of the army, the
meanest private pitied his general: "Ah,
he is a great general, and I am only a
poor private; but I would not exchange
my coarse robe for his magnificent uni-
form, *for he is a leper!*" As he stood in
the brilliant court, at the right hand of
the king, the very doorkeeper beheld
him with disgust: "Ah, he is the favorite of the king, and I am a menial; *but
he is a leper!* I am glad I am not in his
place."

It is wonderful that a man could live
with such an intolerable burden ever on
him. The future had no hope for him.
Steadily, relentlessly, the accursed spot
would spread; there was no cure; his
very bones would rot; his fingers would

at last drop from his hand, and his whole body become a loathsome mass of living, walking corruption. Ah! well may you shudder and grow faint as you look on such a picture; well may you thank God that such a dreadful malady is unknown in this favored land.

And yet Naaman the leper is a representative man: the world is full of such; there are thousands all around us, infected with the moral leprosy of sin, under the curse of God, unclean in their moral nature, excluded from the love and fellowship of God, in different stages of moral disease; but all infected with this hopeless, incurable malady, of which the leprosy is only the type—the deadly, progressive, loathsome disease of sin.

There is an analogy between the leprosy of the body and that of the soul, which it is interesting to trace. Both diseases are hereditary, progressive, incurable by human means, and fatal in every case not divinely cured. The leprosy spared no class, no age, no condition in life. It was not the production of degradation, or poverty, or vice. This great general of the Syrian armies, this favorite of the monarch, this man of noble courage and high renown, was infected with the fatal and loathsome malady. So sin is a universal disease: it is not confined to any one class of men. Sin generic, is universal—the moral nature of our race has a taint in it, which shows itself in a greater or less degree in every child of Adam. There may be specific forms of sin which are not universal; ranker growths of depravity, which attain to monstrous size and fearful appearance; but the taint is in the race of man, and the disease will show itself in all. You may go into cer-

tain parts of our city, and find exhibi-
tions of vice as loathsome and disgusting
as the worst stages of the leprosy; yea,
a perfect moral rottenness that is fearful. But it only shows that the restrain-
ing influences which have surrounded us
all our lives, and which have kept down
the ranker developments of our sinful
nature, have not operated there, and so
our sinful brothers and sisters have gone
farther and faster than we in the progress of sin. They have not a different
original nature from ours; but the mys-
terious discriminations of Providence
have surrounded them with circumstances
more favorable to the rapid and fearful
development of the tainted nature. Had
we been born and nurtured under the
same dreadful influences, should we have
been purer or better than they? Sin is
not a thing of low life nor vicious train-
ing merely. Naaman was a gentleman,

and a rich and titled man, and every thing which high station and elevating influences could do for him was done; yet he was a leper—an incurable leper— just as truly as if he had been the lowest and meanest slave that crouched at the feet of any Syrian lord. And so the word of God and human history and observation—ay, and our consciences— tell us that sin is not a thing of class, or of condition, or of rank; but a taint as universal as the race. It is found in high places as well as in low places: the sinful heart beats as truly under the ermine of the king as the rags of the beggar; wealth has its sins as well as poverty; gentility as well as baseness; learning as well as ignorance; the mansion as well as the cellar; the Fifth-avenue as well as the Five Points.

Men think and feel very differently about sins in high places and those in low; but *God* does not. In fact, our Lord was more severe in his condemnation of the sins of learning, wealth, station, and gentility, than of those in humbler and baser spheres. "The hypocrisies of religion, the impostures of learning, the gilded shows of wealth gotten by extortion, the proud airs of authority and power employed in acts of oppression, provoked His indignation, and he dealt with them in such terms of emphasis as indicate the profoundest possible abhorrence."

But it is a difficult thing for persons situated as you and I are, to get a true idea of the universality and wickedness of sin. We are under the influence of our associations to a great degree; and we judge of moral questions according to the sphere in which we move. The rankest growths of vice do not often meet our eyes; our daily paths do not

lead us into its lowest haunts; many
of us know scarcely any thing of their
existence, but by occasional report.
The most flagrant and revolting forms of
evil do not lie in our sphere, and we
therefore are in danger of lightly es-
teeming the nature of which they are
only the ranker development. And
further, we are apt to confound sin with
vice, and to think that where there is no
positive *vice*, no outward acts of personal
wrong, there is no sin; but this is a terrible mistake. Every thing which we
can say or do, which is not regulated by
Christian principles, is sin.

It was not needful to make a man a
leper, that the disease should have gone
all lengths and corrupted his entire system; and so, to prove us sinners, it is
not needful that we be guilty of a solitary overt act of moral wrong. You see
a farmer quietly ploughing his field; you

say he is pursuing his lawful calling in an honest and laudable diligence. But the Bible says, "The ploughing of the wicked is sin." You see a man come to church, and sit reverently there during the worship; and you say he is doing a right thing. The Bible says, "The prayer of the wicked is an abomination to the Lord." It is a sad, stern fact that, until the heart is right with God, until the man is brought under the influence of religious principles, sin mars his whole character. He may not be guilty of a single vice; but he is not right with God, his nature has the leprous taint in it, and it is not pleasing to God. And never until that taint is removed by the Spirit of God, can he be free from the name and the condemnation of a sinner, though he be among the most respectable, amiable, and lovely of men.

There is an illustrious instance of this

in the case of the young man who came
to Jesus, asking what good thing he
should do to obtain eternal life. He
was a most exemplary character. He
had kept all the commands of the law
from his youth up. He had never done
a vicious act. So very pleasing was he,
so amiable and good, that we are told
that Jesus loved him. And yet when
the probe was pushed down to the bottom of his heart, the taint of the leprosy
was there. His darling sin was discov-
ered, and when he felt the test which, in
his case, revealed his true character, he
shrunk away, and turned his back on
Christ—"he went away sorrowful, for
he had great possessions."

And so this great general, with this
terrible plague-spot upon him, is a representative man. The description given
of him applies to too many of us. We
need not go down into the dark and

filthy dens of vice to find sinners with
the taint of moral leprosy in their blood.
In happy homes; in respectable and
polished social circles; in honorable
business communities; among scholars
and philosophers, and poets, and profes-
sional men; among rulers, and judges,
and legislators—everywhere we find the
leper, with the fatal spot upon his brow.
There is an upright, diligent, honorable
merchant; *but he is a leper;* his heart is
not right with God. There is a moral,
church-going man; *but he is a leper.*
There is an ingenuous youth, the pride
of his parents and the favorite of his
companions; *but he is a leper.* There is
a fair maiden, interesting, accomplished,
intelligent, welcome everywhere; *but she
is a leper.* There is no vice among all
these; there is much that is attractive
to our natural sympathies, and deserv-
ing of our human regard. The leprosy

has not assumed its most virulent form, or presented its loathsome features; but it is there; the taint is in the system. Look down into the heart. Is there Christian principle there? Is there sorrow for sin? Is there love to God? Is there faith in the Lord Jesus Christ there? If not, then the heart is not right; it is not in a healthy state. Sin is there; and sin cannot be the principle of the heart, and yet all be well with the soul. Remember what was said of Naaman: "He was a great man with his master, and honorable; . . . he was also a mighty man of valor; *but he was a leper. Oh dreadful qualification!* It is no slight disease, of little consequence. It is a terrible malady, whose end is death. So it is with you, if you are not a Christian. We may make out the list of all your naturally pleasant traits; we may dilate on your amiable instincts, your kindness, your generosity, your excellence of every kind in the relations of life; but when we have gone through with all, we must add with sorrow, with anxiety, with tears, BUT *he is a sinner— she is a sinner*.

And to be a sinner, is to be under the wrath of God, and in danger of ETERNAL DEATH.

II.

THE CAPTIVE MAID

And the Syrians had gone out by companies, and had brought away captive out of the land of Israel a little maid; and she waited on Naaman's wife. And she said unto her mistress, Would God my lord were with the prophet that is in Samaria, for he would recover him of his leprosy. 2 KINGS 5 : 2, 3.

WE are now introduced to the second personage mentioned in the story of the Syrian leper. She is as obscure as the first is exalted. He is a general and a nobleman; she is a captive and a slave. In one of the forays which the Syrian army had made into the land of Israel, this little maiden had been taken prisoner, and brought in the train of the conqueror to Syria.

Something in her appearance doubtless commended her to the general, and he accordingly selected her as a part of his own household, and she became a waiting-maid to Naaman's wife. Of course, in her new situation she could not long remain a stranger to the terrible malady which afflicted her master, and her youthful heart seems to have been touched with sincere pity for his fearful state. Though she had been torn from her home and her country by him, and reduced to the position of a menial in her conqueror's household, no thought of anger or revenge seems to have entered the gentle bosom of this captive maiden. A base spirit might have exulted in the terrible malady of which Naaman was the victim, and rejoiced in the prospect of his death, as the enemy of her country; but this Hebrew girl manifested a generous and magnanimous spirit. Her quick eye soon saw that a dark shadow rested over the household of the great general; that in spite of his high position and distinguished fame, he and his family were very unhappy. Doubtless her mistress made no secret of her own grief and despair in relation to the miserable condition of her husband; and all this seems to have made a deep impression on the little maid who waited on her. She began to think whether it was possible that he might be cured; she began to feel a very deep interest in the case; she thought of it often and anxiously, until at last she remembered the prophet of her own country, with whose fame she was well acquainted, and the thought came into her mind that it might be that so good and powerful a man as Elisha could heal even the foul disease of the leprosy. It is true she had never known of his doing so, for it is said by our Saviour that though there were many lepers in Israel in the time of Elisha, to none of them was he sent;

but still Elisha had done other things quite as wonderful as this, and so this brave little maid had faith that the prophet of her God and of her native land could recover her master from his foul malady. The more she thinks of it, the greater is her faith and hope; the more she sees of the suffering of the general, who was doubtless a very kind master to her, the deeper does her interest in his case become, until she can no longer refrain from an effort in his behalf. So she goes to her mistress with these earnest words, "Would God my lord were with the prophet that is in Samaria, for he would recover him of his leprosy."

Now this little maid, this humble disciple of the God of Israel in the family of a stranger and a heathen, a "lily among thorns," is set as a fine example to us as Christians in the midst of a sin-

ful and dying world. The great lesson
which she teaches us is, never to lose an
opportunity of doing good in the name
of Christ and for the spiritual welfare of
men. This little maid was placed in
circumstances which, in the judgment of
some, might have excused her from any
effort for the good of those around her.
She was a captive, an exile among the
enemies of her God and her nation; she
had been forcibly abducted from her
country and home, placed in the position of a menial in the house of her captor, and subjected to all the trials inci-
dent to such a position. Surely it is a
work of supererogation to expect her not
only to reconcile herself to her unfortunate situation, but actually to seek for
opportunities to benefit those by whom
she was thus detained in captivity. Yet
this little maid, who seems to have had
a character beyond her years, appears

to have accommodated herself wonderfully to her trying position. She was not sullen or vindictive, or even impatient. She seems to have been respectful to her master's family, and had doubtless gained their confidence and regard by her gentle and exemplary deportment. All her duties were attended to, all the services required of her were cheerfully rendered; and though her heart doubtless often yearned for her home and her people, yet she evidently accepted the situation in which she found herself placed, and determined to make the best of it. And herein she showed her wisdom and her piety; and her example in this respect is a good lesson to us.

It is a rare thing to find people contented with their position in life, even if it be one of comfort and repute. There is always something which we wish were otherwise, something which grates upon our feelings, and provokes an impatient and often a rebellious spirit. We look at others, and wish that our lot was like theirs. Our crosses are heavier, and more vexatious and wearing than those of others; our opportunities are less, our hinderances greater. We spend much time, if not in actual complaint, at least in vain castle-building and imaginings of what we might be and do, if circumstances were changed. Nothing is so utterly vain, and foolish, and wicked as this. The providence of an all-wise God has ordered our lot, and ordained all its conditions. We cannot alter it if we would. Except so far as the doing or neglecting of our duty may affect our condition, we are not responsible for our sphere, but only for our fidelity in it. How much misery would be saved in this world if people would only be content to accept the allotments of Providence, and make the best of their situation. It was a wise saying of the famous Sidney Smith, that people who desire to go cheerfully and hopefully through their work in this life should "take short views;" that is, they should not always be looking far ahead, and fearing some evil to come. Yet it was only an echo of that saying of the wisest and best of teachers, "Take no thought for the morrow," etc. Yes, my friends, whatever be the lot to which Providence appoints us, let us accept it and make the best of it. Let us live on daily bread, and *for* daily duty. The little maid in the home of the Syrian general preaches to us a good lesson on contentment in our lot.

But this is not the main lesson which we learn from this part of the history. As I have already said, the great lesson is, that we are to seek for opportunities of doing good in the sphere where Providence has placed us. There are many persons of kind hearts, and quick sympathies, and active minds, who accomplish but little in the world, because they do not look out for opportunities for doing good where Providence has placed them. They are hoping for a wider sphere, for more enlarged opportunities; they think that their present position is so limited that they can do nothing of any consequence, and so, because they cannot do great things, they do nothing. Now, there is no sphere in life which is utterly barren of openings for usefulness; there is something for everybody to do in this world who has a willing mind; and if it is nothing more than giving a cup of cold water to a thirsty child, it shall not lose its reward. Life is made up of little things; and small opportunities of doing good and making others happy are not to be despised. Suppose you can enliven some poor soul's dull day by one ray of sunshine; that is worth something, and will repay you for the effort. Yes, very little things may cast a bright ray over a cheerless road, and make it pleasanter for a time to the weary traveller.

In going down the Sixth-avenue once, I was attracted by a ragged, hungry-looking little girl looking most intently into a confectioner's window at the tempting array of such things as all children love. Her gaze was so sharp, and there was such an expression of longing on her thin face, that I stopped involuntarily to watch her. I stepped up to her side, and asked her which of all the delicacies in the window she would like the most, if she could have it. She looked at me with an air of timid wonder, and only stared as if she did not know what to make of such a question. I repeated it; but it was only at the third question that she ventured to point, in a very doubtful and timid way, at a certain piece of pastry. It was soon in her hands; and the remembrance of that happy, wondering look went with me through all the work of that day. The tart was a luxury to her, and *that* was a luxury to me. Everybody can do little kindnesses, if they have *no great* opportunities. And if every one did what he could, what a different world this would be. If we all had the spirit of the little captive maid in the Syrian general's house, how much would be done for all kinds of lepers, such as the world is full of.

But the main lesson is to Christians, to those who are the pledged followers of the Lord Jesus Christ. The members of Christ's church are placed here in

this sick and dying world, as the Hebrew maiden was in the Syrian leper's
house, that they may be messengers of
healing, and life, and salvation. I fear
that this does not always present itself
as a great fact to the perceptions of all
Christians. There is a common view of
the church which presents it as a har-
bor of rest for the individual soul. Toss-
ed often, as on a stormy sea, with a
sense of sin, of duty undone, and God
offended, and eternity imperilled, the
soul looks to the church as a haven of
rest, a place of peace, and comfort, and
hope for itself, where the stormy waves
of a reproachful conscience do not beat,
but where there is a great calm for the
believing spirit sheltered from the wrath
of God. But this is a very superficial
view of the church, and of the responsi-
bilities of a Christian state. A sense
of pardon does bring peace. The feel-

ing of being in covenant with God
and his church is a pleasing and happy
one.

But the church is not a place of selfish
repose and enjoyment. It is the family,
the school, the vineyard, the army of
the Lord. Christians are to be obedient
children, diligent scholars, faithful la-
borers, and valiant soldiers for Christ
and his cause. Christ's prayer for his
disciples was, "I pray not that thou
shouldest take them out of the world,
but that thou shouldest keep them from
the evil." Why not take them out of
the world? Heaven is better than earth;
home is better than exile; perfection is
better than imperfection. To depart and
be with Christ is far better. True, when
the time comes; but the world cannot
afford to spare God's people yet. That
pious mother is needed in her family to
train those children for God. That

Christian man is needed to help sustain the great enterprises of Christian benevolence. That teacher is wanted in the industrial and Sabbath school. That Bible-reader is doing a good work among the ignorant and the poor. If all God's people went home to glory as soon as they believed in Christ, how beggared the world would be. Imperfect as the church is, the world cannot afford to lose her. Let us have ten righteous men at least, to save the city. That little maid had her mission in the land of the stranger, and it was a great mission too for such little means. So every Christian has his work—work for his Master, work for his own soul, work for the souls of others. This is the great lesson of this history: Christians are to work for the Lord in laboring for the spiritual good of men. The world is full of lepers, worse than even Naaman himself; and it is the duty of Christians to labor for their cure. Think of this, Christian men and women.

This city is full of moral lepers; they are covered with the plague-spots: what are you doing that they may be healed? They are not out of your reach. You meet them every day; you ride with them in the cars every day; you buy and sell with them; you visit them; you eat and drink with them; you discuss with them the news of the day; you do every thing but try and lead them to Jesus. You know that they are not Christians; that the wrath of God is upon them; that death may find them unprepared at any moment; that unless they go to Christ, they must be lost. Are you doing any thing to help them? What can you do? Do what this little maid did. She spoke of the prophet of the Lord that was in Samaria. Can't

you do as much as this? If your friend
is sick you are ready enough to recommend a remedy for his body, even
though you cannot be sure that it will
relieve him. Can you not recommend
to his soul a Saviour who you *know*
will cure the disease of sin. "Perhaps
he will not take it kindly." Do n't believe it. He wonders why you do n't
sometimes speak to him about religion.
He is ready to meet you half-way.
There are very few men who will not
receive a proper suggestion from a Christian friend in a kind spirit. It is a sad
thing that there are so many who never
hear it, except from the ministers of religion. Oh for the spirit of this little
maid in all our churches! Oh that the
dumb spirit could be driven out of
Christians, and that they could speak
to their fellow-men about the great salvation. It is not strange that men

should be so careless of themselves, when we are so careless of them.

The history of all true revival seasons proves that when Christians are faithful in laboring for the conversion of their impenitent friends, many precious souls are brought into the kingdom of God. The promise of God is, "Ask, and ye shall receive." "Bring ye all the tithes into the storehouse, that there may be meat in my house, and prove me now herewith, saith the Lord of hosts, if I will not open you the windows of heaven, and pour you out a blessing, that there shall not be room enough to receive it." If we desire the salvation of men, we must work for it. The spiritual harvest cannot be reaped any more than the natural, without seed-sowing and cultivation. You cannot secure for your children food and raiment, education and accomplishments, without labor. Can you expect to

secure for them the riches of God's grace
and the treasure of a Christian hope,
while you do not seek them at God's
willing hands by prayer and toil?

Take then, my brethren, this little
maid as your model. A captive in the
land of the stranger, she sought for opportunities of doing good to others and
bringing glory to the God of Israel.
She could not see her conqueror and
captor with the fatal spot of the leprosy
upon him, without an earnest desire for
his cure. And she was not satisfied
with the mere desire, she rested not till
she had spoken to her mistress of that
great prophet of Israel, who might be
able to cure her master. O faithful little
maiden! She shall be honored as long
as the Bible is read. And who cannot
do as much as this? Who cannot point
one sinful soul to the Great Physician?
Who cannot at least express a kind wish

that some impenitent friend would seek the salvation of his soul. Depend upon it, my friend, every honest effort, however humble, which you make for the spiritual welfare of your fellow-men will cheer you in the hour when you must look back on all your earthly life, more than all the successes and gains which have excited the admiration or the envy of the world; for "he which converteth the sinner from the error of his way, shall save a soul from death, and shall hide a multitude of sins."

III.

THE CURE SOUGHT

And one went in, and told his lord, saying, Thus and thus said the maid that is of the land of Israel. And the king of Syria said, Go to, go, and I will send a letter unto the king of Israel. And he departed, and took with him ten talents of silver, and six thousand pieces of gold, and ten changes of raiment. And he brought the letter to the king of Israel, saying, Now when this letter is come unto thee, behold, I have therewith sent Naaman my servant to thee, that thou mayest recover him of his leprosy. And it came to pass, when the king of Israel had read the letter, that he rent his clothes, and said, Am I God, to kill and to make alive, that this man doth send unto me to recover a man of his leprosy? Wherefore consider, I pray you, and see how he seeketh a quarrel against me. And it was so, when Elisha the man of God had heard that the king of Israel had rent his clothes, that he sent to the king, saying, Wherefore hast thou rent thy clothes? let him come now to me, and he shall know that there is a prophet in Israel. So Naaman came with his horses and with his chariot, and stood at the door of the house of Elisha. 2 KINGS 5 : 4-9.

E have considered the character of the little maid, her sympathy with the sad condition of her master, and the timely suggestion

which she made to her mistress—that
the famous prophet of her native land
might be able to effect his cure. Though
coming from this humble source, the suggestion was not lost. The anxious wife
repeated it to her husband, and he
doubtless communicated it to his royal
master. It is very evident that the
king of Syria entertained a high regard
for Naaman, and was disposed to do all
that he could to promote his restoration
to health. Yet, ignorant as he is of this
wonderful prophet, the nature of his
power, and how he can be found, he
knows no better way than to send a
courteous embassy to Joram, who was
at that time king of Israel, accompanied
with a magnificent present of money and
rich robes, such as oriental taste would
covet, with the request that the king of
Israel would take measures for the cure
of his favorite commander. A strange

notion this, that the miraculous power
which could save a man from the living
death of the leprosy, waited on the nod
of kings, or could be bought with sums
of gold, or robes of purple. King Joram
knew better than that; and the receipt
of the letter threw him into great per-
plexity and alarm. He is violently excited; he rends his robe, after the Eastern
fashion, and professes to see in this request that he should take measures to
cure a man of the leprosy, a hostile de-
monstration on the part of his neighbor.
The language of the king of Israel plain-
ly illustrates all that has been said of
the leprosy as a deadly and incurable
disease. He directly declares that nothing less than divine power would be
sufficient for the relief of a leper: "Am
I God, to kill and to make alive, that this
man doth send unto me to recover a man
of his leprosy?" Have I the power of

life and death? Does he expect me to do what God alone can do? No; this is a plot to draw me into a quarrel, because I cannot do an impossible thing: "Consider, I pray you, and see how he seeketh a quarrel against me."

Yet this idea of the king of Syria, of the means of the cure of his favorite general did not differ from that which many persons seem to entertain of the way of salvation from the guilt and condemnation of the leprosy of the soul. The man who came to Jesus with the anxious question, "What good thing shall I do, that I may inherit eternal life?" the men who, on another occasion, asked, "What shall we do, therefore, that we may work the works of God?"—the works which God requires as the price of his favor—entertain the same idea. The Syrian king imagined that he could purchase, by a costly outlay through his brother monarch, the cure of his commander-in-chief. Naaman doubtless sympathized in the feeling, and as he carried the magnificent present of his monarch to the court of Israel, fancied that he was carrying what would surely purchase his cure from the prophet through the agency of the king of Israel. And there is many a man now who, if he could purchase the hope of the Christian by drawing his check on the bank, even for a large amount, would gladly do so. Many a man would be glad to insure the eternal salvation of his soul at a large premium, provided nothing else was required of him but to pay the premium. Oh, if stores of wealth and robes of purple, and jewelled crowns, and golden sceptres could save the souls of men from the guilt, and power, and curse of sin; if a mansion in the skies could be purchased on the same terms

as a mansion on earth, there would be
fewer homeless and miserable souls
roaming over the eternal plains, bewail-
ing in ceaseless sorrow and remorse
their folly in neglecting to secure the
cure of the leprosy of sin while their
day of grace remained.

The king of Israel, as we have seen,
was thrown into great consternation by
the reception of the message from the
king of Syria. It is strange that it did
not occur to him that even in his own
dominions there was a prophet of God,
who had done as wonderful things as to
cure the leprosy. Elisha seems to have
been entirely overlooked by Joram at
this crisis. It seems scarcely possible
that he should have been ignorant of
him, although it was not very long since
Elisha began his public ministry; but
Joram was not a man likely to court any
special intimacy with a holy prophet.

Kings have in very many cases, preferred other companions and counsellors
than the servants of God; and these
ancient prophets of Israel had an independent way of saying plain things, even
to monarchs, that were sometimes extremely unpalatable. They were men
of lofty integrity, who would not stoop
to fawn upon a king. They rebuked the
vices of a sovereign with as much freedom as those of a slave.

In fact, there never has been an order
of men who were clothed with such sa-
credness and wielded such influence as
these old Hebrew prophets, of whom
Moses and Samuel were such illustrious
types. They ever were surrounded with
that awful and venerable atmosphere
peculiar to men who were privileged to
have direct personal communion with
God. Their authority was derived directly from the court of heaven, and the

prophet was recognized as the direct
medium of the revelation of the Divine
will.   Passing and repassing, as they
did, freely from each of the kingdoms
into which the nation was divided, those
of Israel and Judah, and exerting a
powerful influence in both, they were
the chief means in preserving not only
the religious faith, but the national unity
of the people. Such an institution as
that of the prophets in the midst of an
oriental people, was the best guarantee
of popular rights, of progress, of liberty,
and public prosperity.   It has been said
of the modern Dervishes of the East,
with all their faults and vices, "that
without them, no man would be safe.
They are the chief people in the East,
who keep in the recollection of oriental
despots that there are ties between
heaven and earth. They restrain the
tyrant in the oppression of his subjects;

they are consulted by courts and by the councillors of state in times of emergency. They are, in fact, the great benefactors of the human race in the East." The ancient prophets of the Jews did for their age, what the freedom of the press does for ours. They were the firm and powerful representatives and supporters of religion, national unity, and patriotism. Public spirit, devotion to popular rights, stern rebuke of national sin, and lofty enthusiasm for the public welfare, were the noble characteristics of the prophetic order among the Jews.

It is easy to see that such an order of men would naturally be a thorn in the flesh to an unscrupulous, despotic, or irreligious monarch; quite as much an object of fear and dislike as John Knox was to Mary Queen of Scots. And this may account for the fact that King Jo-

ram does not seem to have thought of
referring the letter, which caused him
so much annoyance, to Elisha at once.
Many men are unconscious of the *near-
ness* of salvation. But the fact of the
application, and of the discomposure of
the monarch soon came to the knowledge of the prophet; and he sent word
to the court that the king need not be
so much troubled in this matter: that all
he has to do is to refer the applicant to
him, and he shall soon know that there
is a prophet in Israel. We hear in the
very tone of this unceremonious message the ring of the true metal. What
an independent dignity pervades every
word of it: "*Trouble not thyself, O king,*"
is the message of this minister of God.
"The thing which seems so great to thee
is nothing to me. You seem to have
forgotten that there is a prophet of Je-
hovah at hand, who can do what no

royal mandate can accomplish. Let this leprous stranger come to me. I will soon convince him that a prophet of the Lord can do more for him than any Syrian or Israelitish king." This bold message was doubtless a relief to the disturbed mind of the king of Israel, and it was at once communicated to Naaman, who was probably expecting with some impatience the answer to the communication which he bore from his royal master.

So, the story tells us, Naaman came with his horses and chariot, and stood at the door of the house of Elisha. This simple stroke of the pencil paints quite a striking and significant picture. Naaman, you see, travels in great state. Though he was a miserable leper, with whom the meanest of the people would have disdained to change places, he surrounded himself with all the appendages of wealth and rank. The contrast between the equipage and the rider is very great. The gilded chariot, the prancing horses, the princely retinue of servants, cannot blind the beholder to the melancholy fact that the fatal spot of the deadly malady is on the brow of the great Syrian lord, and that all his wealth and pomp, and power, cannot stay the progress of that cursed disease, or prevent him from being an object of loathing and disgust. We do not say that Naaman did any thing wrong in surrounding himself with all these marks of wealth and state. It is often envy or pride that prompts men to sneer at the style in which their neighbors live, or to decry wealth and luxury, as if there must necessarily be something connected with these inconsistent with purity and goodness. But it is, nevertheless, often a sad thing to see a man surrounding

himself with all the splendors of wealth
and rank, with all that can gratify the
lust of the flesh, the lust of the eyes,
and the pride of life; and to know that
this is all that he has, and that death at
any hour may strip him of all these, and
leave his naked soul beggared and bankrupt for ever. When Garrick showed
Addison his fine house and grounds, and
all the treasures of art and gifts of taste
and luxury with which he was surrounded, it was not envy or asceticism, but an
honest Christian pity which prompted
the remark, "Ah, David, these are the
things which make it hard for a man to
die." No thoughtful man, who saw Naaman riding in magnificent display to the
humble dwelling of the prophet, could
have avoided the feeling of true pity for
a man so distinguished of fortune in all
external things, and yet with the seal of
a living death upon his brow. Let the

warning, then, come to all men who are
heaping up wealth; who are surrounding themselves with all the appliances
of taste and luxury; who are building
costly palaces—collecting the gems of
art, and literature, and refined culture
about them, while as yet they are sick
of the leprosy of the soul, and in danger
of eternal perdition. Not that these
things are in themselves wrong or unde-
sirable. Religion does not condemn nor
depreciate them; but they are not the
first and most radical necessity of the
soul; they do not meet its primal needs;
and the contrast between the externals
of a prosperous man as the world es-
teems him, and the condition and pros-
pects of the soul without any treasure
laid up in heaven, is very sad and terrible to Christian thought.

O my friends, with what earnestness
should the cry of the ancient prophet

come to your ears: "Wherefore do ye
spend money for that which is not bread,
and your labor for that which satisfieth
not?" Listen, all ye who have as yet
made no provision for the eternal necessities of the soul, listen to these words
of Jesus: "Take no thought, saying,
What shall we eat, or what shall we
drink, or wherewithal shall we be clothed. But seek ye first the kingdom of
God and his righteousness, and all these
things shall be added to you."

The story, as far as we have review-
ed it, leaves Naaman the leper sitting in
his chariot surrounded by his servants
at the door of the prophet of Israel. Look
at him there. He is a great man; he is
the favorite of a king; he is commander-
in-chief of the royal forces; he has great
military renown, great wealth and influence, and so far as this world can do any
thing to make a man great and happy,

she has done her best for him. To one
who did not know the one dreadful fact
about him, that he was a leper, he might
seem to be at the summit of human am-
bition. But what is he doing in the land
of Israel? Why is he waiting at the
humble door of a man of God? Ah, he
is a sick man, sick of an incurable disease. The physicians of Syria can give
him no relief; the authority of the king,
his own wealth, his power to control a
hundred thousand swords, are worth
nothing to the leper. Unless the obscure
prophet can heal him by a miracle, he is
a doomed man. This is his real position; this his deplorable case; this his
dire, inexorable necessity. At that door
is his only hope. Within that dwelling
is the only man who can give him help.
If he goes away from that door without
the prophet's aid, he goes to his death.
He goes in a fine chariot, with prancing

Gospel Mission is a non-profit organization dedicated to spreading the Gospel of Christ at the lowest possible cost to our customers. Send for our FREE catalog today and compare.

Name _____

Address _____

City, State, Zip _____

Gospel Mission, Box M, Choteau, MT., 59422

horses, and servants all around him; but he goes to a leper's death, and that death will be just as terrible for him as if he were the meanest slave in all Syria. All earthly distinctions vanish at the gate of the tomb. There is no genteel or fashionable way of dying. The great leveller comes just as unceremoniously to the bed of down as to the pallet of straw. There is many a man who is travelling to a sinner's death-bed in a luxurious chariot, and many are going on foot; but it is the same hopeless, fearful place for all.

The avenues have been crowded to-day with pleasure-seekers, turning God's holy day into a season of selfish and ungodly pleasure. Magnificent equipages have swept along, bearing their owners to our beautiful park. Evidences of that wealth and luxury which have already made this young metropolis renowned all over the civilized world, have been presented on every side, a gay, flaunting show. But how sad, to a truly thoughtful mind, is this Sabbath spectacle. How do angels look down upon it? Ah, they see the taint of the leprosy in it all, and they know that many of these Sabbath pleasure-seekers are riding to a sinner's death-bed. These gilded chariots are the hearses of the soul. These ungodly pleasures will plant thorns in the dying pillow. Purple and gold may hide, but cannot eradicate the leprous spot; and unforgiven sin at last insures the death of the soul.

See, then, in the Syrian leper, as he sits in his chariot at the door of the prophet, a picture of yourself, if you are still an unforgiven soul. All the appliances of wealth and rank may be yours; but if your peace is not made with God, there can be no peace for you for ever.

Naaman desired to be cured; but he had no right views, as we shall see hereafter, of the true method of relief. He thought that he could purchase a cure with gold and splendid raiment; but his disease, like yours, could not be healed by human skill. No fee could purchase purity for the leper at any earthly physician's hands, and

"None but Jesus
Can do helpless sinners good."

IV.

THE WRONG WAY

So Naaman came with his horses and with his chariot,
and stood at the door of the house of Elisha. And Elisha
sent a messenger unto him, saying, Go and wash in Jordan seven times, and thy flesh shall come again to thee,
and thou shalt be clean. But Naaman was wroth, and
went away, and said, Behold, I thought, He will surely
come out to me, and stand, and call on the name of the
Lord his God, and strike his hand over the place, and
recover the leper. Are not Abana and Pharpar, rivers of
Damascus, better than all the waters of Israel? may I not
wash in them, and be clean? So he turned and went
away in a rage.　　　　　　　　2 KINGS 5:9–12.

E have reached that point in
the history of the Syrian leper
where we find him at the door
of the prophet, who, as he believed, had
power to heal him of his terrible malady.
Travelling with oriental pomp, with his
chariot and horses, attended by a princely retinue of servants, Naaman doubtless
expected to make a decided impression

upon the humble man of God. He would
have him know that it is no ordinary
person who visits and consults him. It
is the great general of the Syrian army,
the favorite of the sovereign, a rich and
distinguished personage, who solicits the
prophet's aid. He expected to be received with special consideration, and
that all the circumstances connected
with his cure would be of a marked and
extraordinary character. He expected
that Elisha would come out of his house
and greet him with the attentions due to
a person of his exalted rank; that he
would make a careful examination of his
symptoms, and proceed with much for-
mality and with especial religious rites
to invoke the healing power of Israel's
God in his behalf. It is not at all
strange that Naaman should have cher-
ished these feelings and expectations.
All his previous history prepared him

to do so. He had been accustomed to
profound deference from all around him;
he had always been in the habit of command, and he felt naturally enough the
advantages of his position as the favorite
of the king and the head of the army.
That any one should presume to treat
him, General Naaman, with any thing
approaching indifference, and ignore his
claims to special consideration and respect, probably never occurred to his
mind. He was a proud man, and the
deference which was always shown him
as a great military commander, fos-
tered his natural vanity, and rendered
him extremely sensitive to any thing
like a slight, especially at the hands of
any one who moved in a sphere inferior
to his own. He probably also had no
clear views about the nature of the prophetic office, or the way in which his
cure was to be effected. He doubtless

imagined that a great deal of external
and ceremonial manipulation was needed, that especial and imposing forms and
ceremonies would be practised in his
case, and that his very cure would be
effected in a way to gratify his self-love
and make him feel that, though he was a
leper, he was not one of the vulgar sort.

Now you can imagine what a shock to
Naaman's sensibilities, what a rude blow
to all his ideas and expectations, was
the cool and almost indifferent treatment
which he received at the hands of Elisha.
The prophet would not even come and
see him. The great man must wait at
his door, and at last take a brief message
from a servant's lips. Had he been the
lowest slave in the land, he could not
have had a more unceremonious reception. It was very unexpected and very
aggravating, and Naaman could not conceal his sense of offended dignity and

wounded pride. His injured feeling broke forth at once, "I surely thought that he would come out to *me*, and stand, and call on the name of the Lord his God, and strike his hand over the place, and recover the leper." Why, he treats me as if I was nobody. He will not even look at me. I am not accustomed to such unceremonious treatment. And then his prescription too, "Go wash in Jordan!" Wash in Jordan, indeed! Does this prophet think that I only need a bath? If that were all, I would have spared myself this journey. The splendid streams of my own fair Damascus are better than all the waters of Israel. May I not wash in them and be clean? "So," the story says, "he turned and went away in a rage."

Now if there were no graver or more important lessons to be learned from this part of the history, we might see in

Naaman, as he lashed his horses away in wounded pride from Elisha's house, an illustration of one of the commonest peculiarities of our poor human nature. There are very few persons who do not entertain a higher opinion of themselves than others are disposed to entertain of them, and who do not feel more or less aggrieved when they receive less consideration from their fellow-men than they think they are entitled to. The shoot of self-conceit in us is one of most rank and rapid growth, and sometimes, when it is suddenly pruned down by an unexpected stroke, the process, though it may be salutary, is far from pleasant. A good opinion of ourselves often unconsciously increases upon us. We gradually, and often insensibly, come to think quite highly of our own position, or attainments, or influence, and that our opinions carry great weight with

others. Suddenly, unexpectedly, we find
that we are mistaken; something occurs
to show us, so that we cannot help per-
ceiving it, that we are by no means so
highly thought of as we supposed. The
sermon we have just delivered does not
receive as much approbation as we
thought it deserved; the article or the
poem that we wrote is quite severely
handled by the reviewers; the speech
that we flattered ourselves was so elo-
quent or convincing falls dead on the
public ear; the measure of public policy
we advocated fails to secure support;
the person whom we considered our best
and most partial friend makes some de-
preciating remark about us; the office
for which we think ourselves so emi-
nently qualified is given to somebody
whom we think far inferior to ourselves;
and so we are cut down and wounded in
our tenderest part, and we bleed as a

vine that has been severely pruned.
Ah, it is not pleasant, decidedly not.
But let us bear it patiently, my friends;
it is probably the very thing we need the
most. With all the hard rubs we get in
this common sense world, we have all
of us quite enough of self-conceit left.*
It would never do for us to have things
all our own way. It was quite time for
General Naaman to find out that everybody was not under his command. It is
a good thing for us all to have the con-
ceit taken out of us now and then, before it roots itself so deeply in our hearts
that nothing can eradicate it. "Possibly
there is no one who does not think more
humbly of himself now than he did ten
years ago; and if we live ten years
longer, we shall probably think less of
ourselves then than we do now."

But there are other lessons to be

* The Country Parson.

learned from this part of the history. It is very clear that Naaman from the first had no correct notions of the method by which his cure was to be effected at the hands of the prophet. He evidently thought that there was to be a great deal of external form and ceremony in the process, that it might be a long and labored work, and that he might be called to do some great thing before the cure could be successfully wrought. He had no conception of the extreme simplicity of the method, and that all that would be required of him would be just to believe and do what he was bidden to do by Elisha. It is in this respect that he becomes a representative man, and is a type of many who have some desire to be healed of the leprosy of sin, and yet labor under very erroneous views both as to the method of salvation and the requisite conditions to be fulfilled, before they can enjoy the Christian's hope.

The most common and universal error on the subject of the nature of personal religion is, that it is in some sort a great attainment, a long and labored process, involving great efforts and much pains and costly sacrifices—something that is to be reached only after a continued course of seeking and striving. Some persons imagine that it implies much knowledge of religious truth and Christian doctrine; others, that it involves a state of perfect freedom from sin; others, that it can be reached only through a paroxysm of feeling in which the soul is convulsed and agonized with new and overwhelming emotions. The tendency of all these theories is to make religion something afar off, and not near, accessible, and attainable *at once*. So men are tempted to postpone attention to it

till a convenient season comes, which
Satan is always very glad to have them
do; or else they are discouraged and
despondent about the great difficulties
in their way, and honestly imagine that
there is but little use in their endeavors.
Others again imagine that the hope of the
Christian is to be sought by good works
and prayers, and self-imposed labors and
sacrifices. But in all these theories there
is the idea that to become healed of
moral leprosy, to be a Christian, is a
great work; that there is a great deal to
be done; after which the desired peace
and hope and joy may come to the soul.

It is evident that this was the idea in
Naaman's mind when he went to Samaria to consult the prophet of the Lord.
He took a large sum of money with him
and ten splendid robes. He was prepared to give all these, and to submit to
whatever great thing the prophet might

impose as a condition of restoration;
and he was not a little surprised and
disappointed when he found that nothing like this was required of him. He
was willing to pay a great price for a
cure. He would have greatly preferred
to do so. The fact is, he was a proud
man, who would not stoop to accept as
a gratuity what he could purchase with
his own means. This is a natural feeling of the heart, not always an improper
feeling between man and man, but alto-
gether out of place between man and
God; for the simple fact is, disguise it
as we will, repel it as we may, that in
spiritual things we are all bankrupt.
There was not coin enough in the whole
kingdom of Syria to purchase the cure
of a single leper. The power needed
for the work could not be bought with
money. So the influence needed for
man's spiritual healing and salvation

cannot be bought by any means in our power. The powers of the loftiest mind may be taxed to the utmost, the resources of the richest treasury may be drained, the best time of the longest life may be devoted to the work; but the salvation of the soul cannot thus be secured. In this matter God and man do not, cannot meet on equal terms. It is not as buyer and seller, it is not even as employer and laborer, that man and his Maker meet. It is as criminal and sovereign; it is as guilty helplessness and almighty power; it is as undeserving sinfulness and sovereign grace. On one side are weakness, guilt, hopelessness, and unworthiness; on the other are power, purity, goodness, grace. But there is no obligation on the higher side to come to the help of the lower; and no obligation can be created, except by the free impulse of the higher towards the lower.

And yet the lesson of this history is not a lesson of discouragement to the moral leper, who would fain be healed of his deadly malady. God's way of salvation is far easier and freer than man's. All our ideas of religion put it farther from us, and make it more difficult and inaccessible than God's idea. Naaman expected to do greater things than he was actually required to do. He would have complied with much harder conditions than Elisha imposed upon him. He was amazed when the simple message, "Go wash in Jordan," was brought to him. It did not seem possible that this could be all. He felt that it was like trifling with him, and he was indignant that his case did not receive more marked and solemn treatment. So when men are told that to be a Christian need not require the toils, the prayers, the sacrifices, the struggles of years, but that the

precious gift of pardon and salvation
may be had at once, without money and
without price, the simplicity of the thing
staggers them. It seems like telling a
man that he can become learned without
study, or rich without labor. It is for-
eign to all his preconceived notions; it
is contrary to all familiar analogies; it
is so simple that he cannot understand
it. And yet, my friends, almost every
Christian will tell you that he might
have been such long before he was. He
wonders that he did not see before how
near it was, how accessible, how simple.
He might have been healed of his leprosy long before, if he had only gone to
the prophet of God and taken his advice.
The fact is, that in religion men must
simply take God at his word. They
must not be influenced by philosophy,
or science, or worldly analogies. Salvation is not a science to be mastered by

long study—not an estate to be accumulated by patient industry. It is a deliverance, to be gained by an instant compliance with God's terms—a cure worked in the soul by the healing power of Omnipotence, whenever and wherever the patient is willing to trust the divine Physician and follow his commands.

Banish then from your minds, my friends, all merely human theories about your religious state and necessities. If the leprosy of sin is in your system and you need a cure, do not suppose that the conditions of that cure are beyond your reach. It needs no long and painful conflict, any more than it needs any good deeds or righteousness of your own to secure your salvation. All the store of wealth and purple robes which Naaman brought to the king of Israel could not help him. They were as worthless as a beggar's rags. All your fancied goodness, all your studies, all your struggles, all your efforts, every thing which you can call your own, is nothing to God. He sits as a Sovereign on his throne, with the great gift of salvation in his hands. You need it—Oh, how much you need it! Not a starving wretch ever so needed bread; not a shipwrecked sailor clinging to a plank ever so needed rescue; not a dying patient ever so needed a physician's aid as you need the salvation of God. You cannot buy it, you cannot earn it, you cannot deserve it; but you can have it this day, without money and without price. Would you be healed of the leprosy? "Go wash in Jordan." Would you be saved? "Believe on the Lord Jesus Christ, and thou shalt be saved."

V.

THE LEPER HEALED

And his servants came near, and spake unto him, and said, My father, if the prophet had bid thee do some great thing, wouldest thou not have done it? how much rather then, when he saith to thee, Wash, and be clean. Then went he down, and dipped himself seven times in Jordan, according to the saying of the man of God: and his flesh came again like unto the flesh of a little child, and he was clean. 2 KINGS 5:13, 14.

N our last glance at this history we saw Naaman, under the impulse of wounded pride and disappointed expectation, going away in a rage from the door of Elisha. His sense of personal dignity had been greatly outraged by the unceremonious treatment which he had received from the prophet. The prescription for his cure also seemed to him absurdly simple. He was disappointed to find that all his personal greatness, and the magnificent presents which he had brought with him wherewith to secure the interposition of the prophet of Israel, were considered of no account whatever, and that he was sent away to wash himself in the humble Jordan as the only means for the cure of his terrible disease. Probably no man could have been more surprised and confounded by the treatment and the directions which he received; and it is not strange, considering what human nature is, that he should have turned away in indignant disappointment, and determined to have nothing more to do with the prophet or his counsels.

But it happened that his attendants had more wisdom than their excited lord. They remonstrated with him with a respectful familiarity. They told him that, inasmuch as he was willing to do some great thing at the direction of the prophet for a cure, it was not reasonable, it was not grateful to refuse to do a small thing, even though he could not see the connection between that and his relief. If so simple a thing as to wash in the Jordan would really heal the disease under which he suffered, surely he ought at least to make the trial. It would cost nothing, the river was near at hand, and the experiment could be easily tried. Would it not be wise to do so? If his cure could be effected on terms so much easier than he expected, so much easier than he was prepared to comply with, surely there was every inducement to make the trial.

It was a happy thing for Naaman that he had such good advisers. It does not always fall to the lot of great men to be thus guided. Wise counsel, judicious and candid advice, are of priceless value, especially in our religious concerns.

"He that walketh with wise men shall
be wise, but a companion of fools shall
be destroyed."

Naaman listened to the counsel of his
attendants. His own good sense con-
firmed it. He followed the direction of
Elisha. With a simple faith, giving up
all his preconceived notions, humbly
submitting himself to the guidance of
the prophet, he went and bathed in the
Jordan. Seven times he repeated his
ablutions, and at last the plague-spot
vanished from his body, the ulcers were
healed, and with his diseased flesh made
fair and sound as that of a child, he
emerged from the sacred stream a cured
man, a believer in the God of Elisha,
grateful, humble, joyful, and ready to
consecrate himself and all that he had
to the service of Him who had so miracu-
lously delivered him from a living death.

The lessons which might be drawn

from this history are so numerous, that we are embarrassed in selecting such as seem most pertinent and instructive. We are reminded at once of the great danger which Naaman just escaped, of losing the opportunity of a cure of his dreadful malady, by reason of his own preconceived notions of the mode by which he was to be healed, and his unbelief in the simple method which the prophet directed him to pursue. He came very near the loss of his cure. Had he been left to follow his own impulse and the promptings of his own proud heart, he would have died a miserable death. Does his conduct seem strange to us? Has there been nothing like it in our own experience? Have we not ourselves, perhaps many times, resisted as he did God's demands on our simple faith—God's requirement that we should sacrifice our pride, give up all our favorite preconceptions, and submit implicitly to his terms of salvation? The method which Elisha adopted with the Syrian leper is the method which God adopts with his sinful creatures. He demands faith, he exacts submission, he requires obedience; and when the mind is brought into this state of faith and submission, then, and not till then, he exerts his gracious power, and heals the malady of sin.

This course also does our heavenly Father take all through the spiritual history of his children. In Naaman's case, the first strong impression which was made upon his mind was, that neither he nor his royal master could dictate terms to the God of Israel. That course of proceeding which seemed to them most proper, God repudiated, and took his own course, demanding the unqualified submission of the proud Syrian to that alone.

Often in the course of our career we are checked in the same manner with rigorous claims on our submission, until we are brought into the state of having no will of our own, content to be still in the Lord's hands, leaving him to dispose of all things for us, and recognizing in all matters, readily and cheerfully his way as best. This refusal of the God of heaven to be bound by our methods, is a right which the Lord exercises for our good, thus bringing us into a state of affectionate and constant dependence upon him in all things and at all times. Hence we are continually taken at unawares with incidents which we did not expect or could not calculate upon, but the right reception of which serves to hedge up our way when we become prone to wander, and to instruct us well in all the lessons of his school.

Let us be assured, Christian brethren, that from first to last our will must be merged in God's; his method must be our method, his way our way. He means to teach us this—by what he gives, and by what he takes away, in his dealings directly with us, or on us through others; and that Christian has learned the one great lesson of the Christian life, its reality, its beauty, its progress, its comfort, and its triumph, who has learned, even through much tribulation—*to have no will but God's.*

But the lessons of this history are rather for those who are conscious that they have the leprosy of sin in their souls, and are sincerely desirous of being healed; and the first and most obvious is, *the simplicity of the plan of salvation.*

There is often much mystery thrown around the whole subject of the soul's salvation. Men think of religion as a

science, a philosophy, an achievement,
a long and elaborate experience—as
something to be sought, bought, worked
for, suffered for, for years. Just so
Naaman thought about the cure of the
leprosy. He gathered a large sum of
money and much costly raiment, to pro-
pitiate the good offices of the prophet.
He came expecting that his cure would
cost a great deal. He was willing to go
through a long course of remedies for a
cure. Yea, if Elisha had bid him press
red-hot coals against his ulcerated body
and burn the poison out, it would not
have surprised or daunted him. But
how simple it was after all: Go wash in
Jordan, and be clean. Just so simple
is the plan of salvation. All the great
and difficult work is already done, and
the results are now freely offered to
men. What is religion? What does it
do for men? It puts a soul into right

relations with God; it secures the pardon of sin; it begins a new life in the heart; it ransoms man from the bondage of the world. All this is to be done *for*, not *by* the man; and the simple condition is, *repent* and *believe*. The work is indeed a great and glorious one. It involves results which run parallel with eternal ages; but it is not a work to be done by the sinner. It is to be done *in* him and *for* him by a divine power, which works without money and without price. It was just so in Naaman's case. It was a great result which he sought. It was the healing of a deadly malady; it was the new creation of his poisoned and polluted body; it was the changing of those ulcerated tissues into sound flesh; it was the taking away of the hated taint and hateful name of the leprosy from the general of the Syrian armies. It was a great work. The power of the

monarch could not accomplish it; the
prowess of the warrior was not equal to
it; the wealth of the kingdom could not
purchase it. Yet it was all done for
him, in a moment, through his simple
bathing in the Jordan.

Just as simple is the way by which
the salvation of the soul is gained. The
command is not, Go toil for years; go
study profoundly the truths of religion;
go heap up treasure and buy the gift of
God; go practise some wasting penance;
go free yourself from sin and purge yourself from guilt. If this were so, there
would be no gospel, no glad evangel, no
good news for men. The message is
simply, Believe in Christ, and thou shalt
be saved. The needful work is done.
The law which you have broken, Christ
has honored; the guilt which demands
condemnation has been expiated by
Christ; the curse which sin deserves has

been borne by Christ; and now, go wash in atoning blood; believe on the Lord Jesus Christ, and thou shalt be saved.

Intended as is the plan of salvation for the cure of all varieties of cases, offered as it is to all classes and ages, it must be a simple salvation, or it cannot be adapted to all. The great spiritual necessity of man is one and the same; it is the pardon of sin; it is the smile of God; it is strength, comfort, rest, peace in the soul. Every sinner needs this, whether he be in purple or in rags, on a throne or in a hovel, learned or simple, bond or free; and this one simple free plan is for all. There is not one sun to light the palace and another to light the cottage. The same blessed beams gleam on the prison wall as on the turret of the palace. And so, simple as the light of day, the plan of salvation is adapted to all, and the one glad message of life to universal man is, " *Believe, and be saved.*"

This history also teaches us what is the appropriate spirit for one who seeks to be saved from the leprosy of sin.

A humble spirit. Had Naaman continued to cherish that proud sense of his own importance which first characterized him, he would never have been healed of his disease. He seemed to forget that he was a leper, and to remember only that he was the commander-in-chief of the army of Syria. But such distinctions were of little moment in the prophet's estimation. He saw in Naaman only the unhappy leper, smitten and accursed, unable to wipe out by all his effort a solitary plague-spot from his infected body. This is just the position of all men before God. Whatever difference there may be in social position, or the gifts of fortune among men, in our natural character, we stand on a common level in the sight of God. There is none righteous; no, not one. If any man thinks that he has any thing in him which can commend him to the favorable regard of his Maker above his fellow, he is mistaken; "for *all* have sinned, and come short of the glory of God." All men are not as bad in actual transgression as they might be; and there *is* a great difference in the degree of human virtue, amiable instinct, kindness, generosity, and general loveliness, which are exhibited in human character. But after all, when we get down to that *nature* which is at the bottom, we find that it is a nature morally depraved, unsound, diseased, needing a radical cure, which the Holy Spirit alone can furnish. Naaman was undoubtedly a man of some noble traits; he was a great favorite with his royal master; he was

a brave man; he was a very generous
man; *but* he was a leper. Now we must
discriminate between natural amiable-
ness of temper, kind, generous, manly
instincts and exercises, and radical holi-
ness of heart. And often the abundance
of the one only proves the lack of the
other; for it is not uncommon to see
men who are very well disposed towards
their fellow-men, but very ill disposed
towards God. How many men there
are whom you would call fine, gener-
ous-hearted, whole-souled men, who
never think of God who made and pre-
serves them, and sent his Son to die for
them—who never have a thought of
gratitude, or love, or obedience for him
to whose goodness they owe their all.
Is not this a monstrous state of things?
Is there no moral depravity there? I
tell you, badly as men have sometimes
treated their fellow-men, the worst-

abused man on earth was never so much abused as the great and good God is every day by creatures on whom he is pouring the continual dew of his blessing.

When a man comes to God for salvation, he must come with a sense of ill-desert. He must not come in his chariot, with all the trappings of pride about him; but he must come on his knees, smiting his breast, and saying, "God be merciful to me a sinner." He must not come with money and fine robes, expecting to be saved in return for his good deeds. He must come in poverty and nakedness of spirit, feeling that he is wretched and miserable and poor and blind and naked, and in need of all things. Only thus can he find a free and full salvation.

We are also taught that salvation must be sought *in a believing and obedient spirit.*

We may have our own notions about the
mode; but we must give them all up,
and accept God's mode, no matter how
perplexing it may be to our reason or
humbling to our pride.   It is not reason
so much as faith that we need.   Naaman
could not see how just washing in the
Jordan could heal his leprosy; and because it seemed to him unreasonable, he
was inclined to refuse to do it.   But the
mode of salvation is revealed to our
faith, and all that God asks of us is to
believe and obey.

"It is extraordinary," says a quaint
English preacher,* "how different are
the conclusions of faith from those of reason.   Once Reason came along, and she
heard a man cry, 'I am guilty, guilty.'
She stopped, and said, 'The man is guilty.
God condemns the guilty; therefore this
man will be condemned.'   She went

* Spurgeon.

away, left the man condemned, ruined,
and quivering with fear. Faith came
and heard the same cry, rendered more
bitter by the cruel syllogism of Reason.
Faith stopped; she said, 'The man is
guilty. Christ died for the guilty; the
man will be saved.' And her logic was
right; the man lifted up his head, and
rejoiced. Reason came one day and
saw a man naked, and she said, 'He
hath not on a wedding garment. Can
naked souls appear before the bar of
God? Should they have a place at the
supper of the Lamb? The man is naked; he must be cast out, for naked
ones cannot enter heaven.' Then Faith
came by, and said, 'The man is naked.
Christ wrought a robe of righteousness.
He must have made it for the naked;
he would not have made it for those
who had a robe of their own. That
robe is for the naked man, and he

shall stand in it before God.' And her
logic was right and just. Reason one
day heard a man say that he was righteous and good. She saw him go up to
the temple and pray, 'Lord, I thank
thee that I am not as other men.' Said
Reason, 'That man is better than others,
and he will be accepted.' But she ar-
gued wrongly; for lo, he went out, and
a poor sinner by his side, who could
only say, 'God be merciful to me a sinner,' went down to his house justified,
while the proud Pharisee went on his
way disregarded. The logic of Faith is
to argue white from black, while the
logic of Reason argues white from white.
Luther says, 'Once upon a time the
devil came to me, and said, 'Martin Luther, you are a great sinner, and you
will be damned.' 'Stop, stop,' said I;
'one thing at a time. I am a great sinner, it is true, though you have no right

to tell me of it. I confess it. What
next?' 'Therefore you will be damned.'
'That is not good reasoning. It is true,
I am a great sinner; but it is written,
'Jesus Christ came to save sinners;'
therefore I shall be saved. Now go
your way.' So I cut the devil off with
his own sword, and he went away mourn-
ing, because he could not cast me down
by calling me a sinner.'"

Every man has a right to believe that
Jesus died for him, if he casts himself
upon him. Every drop of Jesus' blood
says to the true penitent, "*I was shed
for you.*" He has nothing to do with
any method of his own. He is full of
leprosy. Here is a cleansing stream.
All he has to do is to believe, and wash.
Wash in Jesus' blood, and the leprosy
is cured, and cured for ever. Eighteen
hundred years have heard only one answer to the question, What must I do to

be saved? It is this, "*Believe on the Lord Jesus Christ, and thou shalt be saved.*"

To recapitulate then the lessons of this whole history. We see in it, first, a picture of the natural condition of man. He is a sinner. However exalted in position, however gifted with endowments, honored by others, and favored by the world, the taint of this leprosy of the soul is on him, and unless he is cured, he must perish for ever.

Next, we see in the history of the little maid, how Christians ought to feel and act in reference to their sinful fellow-men, taking the liveliest interest in their case, and seeking in every way to direct them to the almighty and loving Saviour.

Next, we are taught that it is the duty of every sinner to seek at once the salvation of his soul; and we are warned against all false theories of religion, which may lead us to seek it in the wrong way.

Lastly, we are instructed as to the simplicity of the gospel plan, and the true spirit in which a sinner should come to the Lord Jesus Christ.

May God bless to all of us our study of this interesting narrative, lead us all to the fountain of purity and life in the blood of Jesus, and gather us all at last, washed, purified, and healed of the leprosy of the soul, into the everlasting paradise of the saints.